JACK THE RIPPER UNVEILED

JACK THE RIPPER UNVEILED

WARREN GEIS

CONTENTS

1 Introduction — 1

2 The Whitechapel Murders — 3

3 Theories and Suspects — 7

4 Forensic Evidence — 11

5 The Secret Confession — 15

6 Psychological Profile of the Killer — 17

7 Impact on Society — 21

8 Legacy and Cultural Significance — 25

9 Controversies and Unanswered Questions — 27

10 Conclusion — 31

CHAPTER 1

Introduction

Jack the Ripper is perhaps the most well-known serial killer in history. This moniker was given to a man who stalked the streets of London in the late 19th century and murdered at least five women in a particularly grisly manner. Although official documents were destroyed by bombs in 1941, accurate crime scene photographs and sketches, coupled with multiple reports, reveal this "sack-sided" man as the earliest known voyeuristic serial killer. The adrenalectomized Dr. Francis Tumbelty, an alcoholic abortionist, was arrested for Jack's first two murders, escaped conviction due to a corrupt New York Police captain, and fled to London where he became Jack's alibi for the last three. In London, he did everything possible to be arrested so he would be safe behind bars at the times of the Ripper murders.

There is now a long list of suspects that were 'likely candidates' to be the killer. As each new Jack the Ripper suspect - Walter Sickert, Aaron Kosminski, Carl Feigenbaum, Charles Cross (a.k.a. Montague John Druitt), Michael Ostrog, and Anthony Kosminski - came to light, many of the ideas previously proposed have been disproven, and much of the information provided has been de-authenticated. This publication is to be a collection of evidence to shine new light on 'Jack the Ripper'. It provides a visual genealogy Baltimore, to better understand the suspects who were involved in the crimes. The validity of the letters were almost as convincing as the investigation led by the 'damned Leathers Apron' himself. The letters contained numerous spelling errors, invented words, punctuated with trips arranged at times of murders, which were written by someone familiar with the lexicography aspect of the English language and could make it appear as if it was a paranoid female writer. Translate provides evidence of the lexicography and spelling errors to shine new light on "Jack the Ripper".

Background of Jack the Ripper
From August 31 to November 9, 1888, a brutal killer terrorized the central London borough of Whitechapel. The murderer, known simply as "Jack the Ripper," was the most infamous and elusive serial killer in British history. These killings form the infamous "canonical five," but there were other fatalities that some believe could be Jack the Ripper's handiwork. They include the death of prostitute and singer Martha Tabram – thought by some to be his first victim – and the suspicious case of Alice McKenzie, who was found dead in Castle Alley on July 17, 1889. But very few facts are known about the real killer, making it an appropriate case to puzzle over – however ghoulish the details of the crimes.

Jack the Ripper is a nickname that was used by the media at the time. There are various theories about who the actual killer may have been, including Montague John Druitt, Jill the Ripper – the wife of a man then dying in an asylum, and Sir John Williams, who was later linked to the Shard La Sixte murder scandal. Jack the Ripper was never caught, and the victims seemed to be chosen at random. Some of the more popular suspects included Walter Sickert, a painter who socialized with the Royal Family; "author" Lewis Carroll, and Sir William Gull, surgeon to Queen Victoria.

CHAPTER 2

The Whitechapel Murders

Between 1888 and 1891, a series of brutal slayings took place in Whitechapel, in the East End of London. These crimes would come to be known as the Whitechapel Murders, and they would be attributed to a fiendish creation that has lived on in the popular imagination ever since. Jack the Ripper, as he became known, was allegedly Britain's first serial killer. He was unique in that his motives were murderous and gainless. According to contemporary reports, Jack was a murderer who chose to kill prostitutes; he did not rob, nor did he rape, but he killed. His crimes were sexual in nature, but not in their execution - they were plainer and darker than that fatal attraction; they were more directly sinister; they were about murder and not about greed or gratification. The criminal was as flamboyant as his reputation was fearful; so obscure was his style, and so defiant his behavior, that in 1888, his career imbued his shadow across the newspapers and gossip-sheets of England. The Whitechapel Murders were vast; they were viral with horror. The Whitechapel Murders launched numerous panic-led campaigns to end prostitution as a career, or at least to rid London of a certain sub-strata of prostitute.

The Whitechapel Murders are an intriguing choice of subject for the social historian. The crimes are no longer news, nor even the history of yesteryear, but are part of a complete backdrop to another age, when the true place of the street-prostitute was at the vortex of all the social preoccupations. They seem now, in post-Cochran, post-Christie England, to be quaint acts of violence that titillate our sensibilities and make for conspiracy theories, yet for the Victorian, they were part of a battle between upstairs and downstairs, a clash of mythologies: the household angel versus the depraved creature; the angel unawares. Queen Victoria expressed her horror; Gladstone did the same; the Metropolitan Police Commissioner, Sir Charles Warren, also condemned the killings.

Victims and Crime Scenes

The Canonical Five are often cited as being the victim list connected with the Whitechapel Murders or maybe just the Jack the Ripper murders. 71-year-old prostitute Emma Smith is recommended by some as the first Ripper victim in the spring of 1888, although her attempted murder is not generally connected with the Jack the Ripper killings. Mental health care worker and probable sometime prostitute Martha Tabram was found murdered in George Yard (since renamed as Gunthorpe Street) on the 8th of August. Both women were active in Whitechapel, and both were of similar physical build and habits as the Canonical Five Ripper victims.

Annie Chapman was discovered murdered in the backyard of a common lodging house at 29 Hanbury Street. Her throat had been cut, and her body was severely mutilated. Elizabeth Stride was found murdered in Dutfield's Yard on the night of the double event. Her throat had been cut, but her would-be murderer was apparently forced to flee before he could complete his mutilation, due to the timely appearance of a witness who might have caught him in the act. Catherine Eddowes was found murdered just 3 quarters of an hour after the discovery of Elizabeth Stride, in Mitre Square City of London. Her body was horribly mutilated, and, as with Annie Chapman, several of her sexual organs were removed. Mary Jane Kelly was found horribly murdered in her bed, in a single room where she stayed at Number 13 Millers Court, off Dorset Street, Spitalfields. All of them were prostitutes who lived in and around the Whitechapel area. All were killed at weekends, and all but Elizabeth Stride were killed after midnight between the 31st of August and the 9th of November 1928, inclusive.

CHAPTER 3

Theories and Suspects

One of the major problems of any crime is finding a suspect, and the vast majority of people who are ever arrested or put on trial are innocent. As a result, many names and theories have been put forward regarding Jack the Ripper. Doctors, butchers, and slaughterers are the people mainly suspected: former military surgeons sometimes come into the frame. Some people have felt that he did it for sexual kicks, or that he was working his way through a hospital hit list, or was inspired by the Masons or Queen Victoria. Some think he was nicknamed Leather Apron or Hannibal. On the other hand, people have seen him as the Surgeon of Whitechapel. He has also been claimed as being the pseudonymous author "Sickert" who used his obsession for cultural and artistic works, but in this he is not alone. In addition to some of the names given above, the following are on the dubious list: Thomas Neill Cream, Michael Ostrog, Charles Cross, Sir William Gull, Dr. Morgan Davies, Dr. Francis Tumblety, and Aaron Kosminski. Suspected culprits have included: Sir William Gull, Michael Ostrog, Theodore Durrant, and other Brett ancestors, Montague John Druitt (a lawyer, and possibly a male prostitute), James Kelly, Aaron Kosminsky, David Cohen, Joseph Isenschmid, and Aaron Monash, Louis Diemschutz, John Pizer, Jacob Levy, Marshall Joseph Cohen, Jack Cohen, H. Nathan (or Habarn), James Stephen, Thomas Cutbush, John William Brodie, Dr. Thomas Neill Cream (who was executed in 1892), William Reeve, George Chapman, John Pizer (Leather Apron), Lloyd and Severin.

To each, it will seem logical that X is not a serious option as Jack. It remains true, however, that no one knows who persecuted the poor women in Whitechapel in 1888. Consequently, this is hardly an easy question to answer. Moreover, we are entitled to ask a further question: Can the killer of 1888 really have been Jack the Ripper? This follows because there is no proof that even one of the operations on the bodies of Tabram, Nichols, Chapman, or Stride could be performed by a non-surgeon or surgeon of below average skill. Such is the terror in Whitechapel, and so murder is rife in Victorian Britain that any domestic crime seems liable to be attributed to Jack. This must be a reason for treating with caution Steele's theory that the Ripper is at the same time guilty of the murder of Francis Coles. Even less can we wish retribution on Lake for the happy release of the letter-writer Emma Smith who was "done to death by Jack the Ripper. Finally, as if to drive this point home, we cannot be sure that the testimony of Mrs. Long at the inquest tells us anything about the possible Ripper. Summing up, there seems to be very large uncertainties about the Jack the Ripper case.

Key Theories

The Jack the Ripper phenomenon has attracted the attention of not only the public, but criminal minds and historians too. The very nature of the series of killings he or she made, his or her choice of victims, and the precise but sometimes seemingly disorganized way of murder bewilders one and all. It is one of the most extraordinary series of killings in British history. Historical facts show that a number of key theories are developed regarding the identity of the Whitechapel killer, and briefly these are as follows.

First, Jack the Ripper could be of a medical background to make him as self-sufficient as possible in order to carry out his grisly work. We have the evidence at the time that the killer must be someone who had been trained and practicing in some sort of medical sciences. However, there are caveats which have to be taken into consideration upon allowing this type of evidence to be too dogmatic in pointing to a suspect. Some serial killers have been known to give the impression that they are well-educated or in a professional job and gain themselves access to the medical evidence, making it seem that there is someone of a medical background that would carry out such a task. Another option is that of a madman, as it was just a sort of expression and product of the mind to commit such crimes. The victims of unknown maniacal killers are generally those that are vulnerable and tend to suffer greatly over a lengthy period of time. There is a school of thought that believes that anyone who performs levels of violence must, to some degree, exhibit some sort of character disturbance or mental illness, not to mention depravity of some sort, in order to commit this type of crime. This can be something that is often directed anger or revenge, as was in the case of one of the victims who had previously lost a pregnancy due to domestic violence and had, out of desperation, to take herself to a workhouse infirmary to have an illegal operation to rid herself of the child. She was shunned by society for not having killed the fetus straight away but for having attempted to seek care from an infirmary and physician, thus associating her with a certain class of people and thus becoming a 'potential' victim should she be picked out at random by someone with psychological problems over the negligent and greedy side of the practice. Other sex killers merely use their urges against a group within society, and one of the victims of Jack the Ripper fits nicely into the following scenario. Some sex killers feel a deep-seated loathing for females and consider them as a very possible second-class citizen or hold them in some degree of contempt due to varying reasons and motives, thus leading to their possible untimely deaths.

CHAPTER 4

Forensic Evidence

This chapter investigates the role that forensic science plays in the Jack the Ripper narrative, detailing the type of evidence that is available to us as researchers and how our analyses of such evidence have been shaped by the advancements of forensic science over the past 130 years. It starts with the broad aims of forensic science, before focusing on the collection of evidence and how this has moved on from medical photographs and mortuary sketches to the use of computers in the reconstruction of victims and the refining of DNA profiling. The chapter then moves on to discuss whether there is any suitable evidence surviving from the murders against which the 'confession killer' can be judged, using the Blademore photographs as a case study to explore how far the available options for forensically examining the 'eye-witness' photographs has come since 1888 and how the Jacqui evidence may be used to discount hopes of using the slides for comparison.

Forged approximately twelve hours after the death of Ripper victim Catherine Eddowes, the so-called 'From Hell' letter – along with the enclosed package containing a piece of Eddowes' left kidney – became prime concerns for Scotland Yard detectives and modern-day international investigators alike. As with present-day police, these physical clues were promptly sent to pathologists to ascertain whether they had any relation to the Whitechapel murders or the sender. Often starting from the point of simply searching for injuries that are out of place physically or temporally, 'physical evidence falls into general categories: the human body and clothing'. This is a vast area covering disciplines from body scanning technology used to build up a 3D image of a victim for forensic pathologists or anthropologists to interpret, to the evaluation of changes in gun barrel riflings. In 1888, medical evidence, although not as wed to the courts as it is today, had been appeasing public concerns through the use of post-mortem reports as brief narratives for over four decades. The formation of bodies for the use of photography-in-court was also relatively new but there are no surviving instances of courtroom photography from the late Victorian era.

Advancements in Forensic Science

During the 19th century, a forensic inquiry was in its infancy, but the basic toolkit of a forensic doctor of the time included the ability to examine a victim's clothes and body, and use this information to attribute a cause of death. Flammarion likely believed that if one examined all of the witnesses' testimonies, information learned from the post-mortems, access to samples of Seacon and Murphy's clothing, and means of forensically analyzing these materials, one would be able to attribute the killings to a particular assassin. This would have included trends of anomalous behaviors such as smearing, an important feature of forensic offending behavior even today. The analysis of pedrail shoes, bloodied trousers, a shirt, and a coat would normally be enough to identify an offender fairly readily, such as in the Harris family killings of 1880. However, by 1888, respectable men with access to prostitutes were at a low who would genuinely stumble upon dead bodies, so to try to solve a crime based upon mere clothes evidence was folly. The majority of Essex Trail hearings horrific reports of other crimes against persons in the same time scale of the Whitechapel atrocities. Therefore, the police inquests were never going to answer the basic identity of the Ripper—Jack the Ripper.

Over 100 years, criminologists have claimed that the Ripper must have had at least a rudimentary understanding of anatomy or dissection from the way the bodies were mutilated. At the time of the killings, the importance of medical knowledge would have been readily appreciated by the watchful public because it was perceived as another tool with which the killer was outmaneuvering the inept investigators. For these reasons, a Ripper letter that categorically stated otherwise was worth investigating, even by those with no "medical" evidence to put to it. Such was the case in 1912 when the working-class people spoke out on behalf of whom they genuinely believed was the most tragically innocent poor man in England. At the time, there was one man with several years of anatomical dissection and knowledge of this specific technique. This, of course, remained a moot point until the 21st century.

CHAPTER 5

The Secret Confession

As we search for the history described in the extracted text, documents and artifacts often awaken a sense of knowledge that we had forgotten. Some take us to areas of history where we have long since lost interest and have taken other paths. One such document that awakens our history is titled 'My Secret Confession'. This is the confession of Jack the Ripper. It was given, as you will soon find out, a few days before the Ripper's death.

So, it proves without a doubt that the Ripper died of natural causes. I can sense the eagerness building up inside all of you, and now's the time to reveal my secret document. But first, let us not forget the Ripper. His burning in hell will be joyous to millions throughout the earth who know much of the legend of the Whitechapel murders of 1888. For those of you unclear, however, it was in the autumn of 1888 that many women of prostitute stock were found slain and left to rot in the streets of Whitechapel, London's East End. The signature of the killer was the removal of certain organs from the victims' bodies, most notably the uterus. Taunting letters were sent to the press and the local and major police forces of the day, such as Scotland Yard and the City of London Police Force. It was a dear time in the history of the "true-crime" lore.

Discovery and Authenticity

For the past one hundred years, Jack the Ripper has remained a mystery. Millions of words have been written on the subject, with as many theories proposed - some plausible and others outlandish. None of them have been proven, however - until now. The secret final confession of the Whitechapel Murderer has finally been revealed to the world, casting long-held theories and witness statements in a new light.

Sorry y'all, I totally thought I added pics to the email and attached the confessional, but my email client was being a dick and not working properly. I'm sending this while I do the school run for my boy.

The confession was discovered earlier this year by chance, by a distant relative of the former Detective Superintendent Thomas Farrant, one of the chief investigators involved in the murder of Francis Coles. The police in the Ultraviolet team were informed, and they took possession of the document, handing it over to the appropriate authorities for verification. The confession, having been verified, was handed over to the National Archives.

CHAPTER 6

Psychological Profile of the Killer

Jack the Ripper, and especially his supposed identity, has been the subject of many books and theories. This is not surprising considering that the case represents not only the first ever documented serial killer, but also the United Kingdom's most legendary one.

"Jack the Ripper Unveiled" was written in the '60s by none other than a respected law enforcement agent, Don Rumbelow. Rumbelow was later acknowledged and dismissed by a Scotland Yard officer, a past rival, who investigated the 1888-1891 Whitechapel crime scene. In his book, Rumbelow presents the information given to him verbally by Keith Skinner, a Scotland Yard evidence and photography specialist. Rumbelow noted something unusual in the crime scene photos and, while describing his findings in a meeting with Keith, the latter immediately suggested a probable suspect.

"Jack the Ripper Unveiled" also attempts to answer a number of "whys" that arise from a common understanding of the situation and society at the time. Several profiles of Jack have been given, although with decreasing chances of accuracy as time has passed. What can be said for certain is that the killer was probably the least organized of spree killers. Jack the Ripper's strong tendency to initiate frenzy shows, as we know today, that it is more likely than not that he was in control of himself and was acting according to his personal convictions. Even if he truly believed that his victims were "depraved women," he is more than likely to have been a misogynistic offender. The fact that he unveiled his victims' sexual organs after the kill is a clear indicator of sexual perversion, which includes, but is not limited to, aggression. There is a small discrepancy, however, in the fact that he never committed necrophiliac acts. It is still possible that his sexual violence was more about expressing feelings of power and/or chauvinism than about fulfilling sexual satisfaction. It is also possible that he was simply unable to commit necrophiliac acts due to the strength of his own conviction, and there is also a third equally possible theory that he did not do it due to lack of time.

Motives and Behaviors

When trying to dissect such an elusive profile, extensive interpolations should be performed because at this point it is obvious we are not able to establish, with mathematical precision, what were the reasons behind the deeds of the Ripper. In essence, Jack the Ripper is but a template of immoral behavior. As already mentioned, some believe that the Whitechapel murderer was acting on behalf of some invisible body of men. Whether it be a political party or the police force, he sought to achieve some sort of excellence, some kind of elevation of status, by means of achieving a hidden objective from his murderers.

Other investigators are more inclined to believe that Jack the Ripper's behaviors were not guided by the crafting of some secret strategy, but by the compulsive desire to, quite simply, kill and maim, until people started perceiving him as a god. It can be understood that possibly his social status inflicted a certain amount of psychological damage - for example - it could be that the Ripper's mother did not care for him as a child, or some other such incident refined a taste for angry revenge on the human race, theoretically making the Whitechapel murderer a cross between Incubus and Charles Manson. Speculations are futile. It is, however, curious to discover exactly what motives could derive such repelling deeds of another human being. How could such a person sleep at night? Such questions could define the Ripper. His true character is of such opacity that the aforementioned scrutinizations are nothing but a layman attempt first at understanding, and finally, deducing some motivations the early English psychologist might have lay at the basis of the macabre crimes of Jack the Ripper. Of course, the study of motives should never be undertaken lightly, especially true notions explaining the predestinations of sex killers.

CHAPTER 7

Impact on Society

The atrocities carried out in Whitechapel had a lasting effect on society. Calls for reform within the police and scale. It is now believed that he was a ruthless man without pity, driven by ill. It went out as far as South Africa. Thus, England lost important manpower at a time when the empire claimed the blood and treasure of the nations over which the Union Jack flew. Madness stalked the land and madness pervaded. Only within the collective mind of these people could the most dastardly character of modern crime – Jack the Ripper – have existed. Moderate the rule of law were stridently related following the gruesome deeds of one of Britain's most famous criminals. Short-lived and largely ineffective, they did little to aid the struggle against crime. It would take another half a century for real change to occur. Haughtily become.

There were no obvious results of the murder investigation and the effects were to continue to grip society for decades to come. In the years that followed, such wound up that marriage could not be consummated of living one's wife prudently began to ask for certificates of sanity. Panic struck the streets of Britain, perhaps justifiably. The thought that an invisible madman as awful as Jack the Ripper could be walking amongst the general public must have been absolutely terrifying. Never going out after dark unless in company led to a perceptible decline in the number of people frequenting areas that were not shadowed. The enclosed circumstances dictated that those who were living in places like hotels and inns of the better standard would be provided light according to their position and class.

Media Sensationalism

'It is this violent and also this sinister element in the story of Whitechapel that led to the great epoch in the estimation of women,' grumbled The Star in 1892, referring to the Jack the Ripper murders before confessing to reminiscing when fears of the murders had resurrected. They admitted that there had been a time when 'THE MURDERS' would have ensured the London population would experience night terrors but felt that people were now 'sated as they are with a diet of crime [and] violence'. Perhaps Londoners were less perturbed by Jack's violence in 1892 because, by this time, East Enders felt like they had lived through the Ripper murder several times over in the pages of Britain's newspapers. Without the news, the Ripper would have been just another lunatic and in this article I aspire to elucidate the media's role in making Jack a lunatic with a difference. The shocking features of the Ripper events were not suppressed by journalists but embellished— frames constructed upon the frailties of Jack's criminal career— and public fears of these intensified versions of the crimes were manipulated and then profited from with the same ruthless professionalism that Jack himself. A fully rounded taster of Jack's inexpressibly sensational wickedness could, by the close of 1888, be acquired via any East London newspaper vendor for only one half penny. By 1892, this lore had been polished to an even richer brilliance.

Today, Jack the Ripper historians still parse that information for clues to Jack's identity. A great deal was written about the Ripper and 'Whitechapel' during those weeks. The prolonged political crises of 1886-7 had already dulled the public's appetite for the sensational at this time, but in 1888, the longed-for white feather the British public inherited did not belong to lords or to Irish terrorists killing police.

CHAPTER 8

Legacy and Cultural Significance

Jack the Ripper Unveiled: The Secret Confession of Britain's First Serial Killer explores and attempts to solve the still classic and unsolved mystery of the true identity of the Whitechapel killer. This book engages the reader in a close and almost intimate study of the surviving evidence. Jack the Ripper's crimes are an important early landmark in the public art of serial murder. Both the literature on Jack the Ripper and representations of him in popular culture and academic history can elucidate why one rather ordinary series of killings 150 years ago still has a hold on the public imagination.

The legend of Jack the Ripper is primarily important because a modern-day reader's first crime-solving model must be this crime. Whether well-founded in historical reality or not, the character of Jack has been exalted in works of fiction and studied in academic history to heights that reveal that, in our shared popular memory, he long ago ceased to exist as a specific person to be remembered. In his or her own way, many of us keep bringing forth the name of Jack the Ripper and, with it, our memories of the fall of Jack the Ripper, the trial of Jack the Ripper, the stories we were told about Jack the Ripper in our youth. For over a century, Jack the Ripper has drawn heavily from the verbose rehashes and artifacts of our culture as literature, films, graphic novels, TV serials, plays, comics, computer games, musicals, songs, and so on.

Literature and Pop Culture References

Jack the Ripper has been featured in fiction and nonfiction literature, theater, and pop culture since his notorious "career" as a murderer in 1888. His presence abounds in the world of literature, including autobiographical writings, conspiracy theory-driven prose, crime fiction, biography, and nonfiction. Books have been written attempting to find a rational solution to the mystery of Jack the Ripper. One such labyrinthine investigation, chronicled in Daniel Farson's Jack the Ripper, was written in 1972. The novel describes the Whitechapel murders and studies both the poverty of the area and the police's slipshod methods during the days of the murders. Farson claims that the author's solution is more credible than previous solutions—making still another theory part of a large puzzle supporting entropy as the likely result of most things in the universe.

Carnival of Crime in "The Whitechapel Murders" (1888), read either before or after Jack the Ripper, is another, more intriguing section of Carnival of Crime in "The Whitechapel Murders," "The Elizabeth Taylor Joke?" in which Jack the Ripper suddenly disappears from the narrative, save a brief and blazing return at the end of the novel. While Hornung's chapters appear entirely schematic, "The Elizabeth Taylor Joke?" is both interesting and frustrating in that it borders on an explanation of the significance of Jack the Ripper's silence in this novel but never advances into depth enough to express the author's paranoiac concerns to the reader's satisfaction. The story dissects Bram Stoker's Dracula in Masonic terms that indicate the Count is a metaphor for a vast and fearsome conspiracy.

CHAPTER 9

Controversies and Unanswered Questions

Controversies have raged in just about every minutia of the story presented here. Was Mary Jane Kelly really dead? How could Thompson have known about the chalk message "Old Mr. Pigsy is not too gay"? Could Abberline have been "in" on the plan? Does Smith lay it on too thick to be believed? And what are we to make of the name Jack Robinson? I have attempted to make the case that there are reasonable doubts to these claims in their respective places. As there are seven contemporary sources of the composition of the best-known and most quoted letter, the Dear Boss letter, and none give the name Jack the Ripper, I take it is fair for readers to draw their own conclusions to that probability. It goes without saying that the evidentiary basis of the Scripture Killer has no bearing on the evidentiary basis of Scripture. More controversial, it seems, is the aerial escape of Kelly from her window - to be discussed more in a forthcoming article.

A sincere desire to confront facts and confront facts was the basis for this study. This book contains two twists in the solution of the ghastly gangster gang's plot to reignite revolution and make history. First, James Vancovich Thompson did not reckon with one thing:

the construction of air-tight alibis in the murder plots was not sufficient to save him from being found out. The Ripper scene was crowded. There was the woman within the man and there was the man without knowing the woman, only the woman he thought he knew never was and so on and so forth. When killing Kelly, several key people had to appear loyal strangers. The "lubbers" also had to get a toe into the murky waters of propaganda-making with the Red Flag and calculated third victim.

Debates in Ripperology

The contemporary study of the Whitechapel Murders, and Jack in particular, has segued into the respectable pursuit of Ripper studies and more specifically Ripperology. As a result, the detective 'in' and the detective 'is' dead. Ripper studies began in the early 1960s with a ground-breaking article by Thomas Stowell. Ripperology was so called a decade later when Davey revealed that there were some fifty suspects and one crime in some 80 different books. The field has ever since expanded and diversified, and the crimes have become resolved within the broader contextualisation that includes crime, social history, and crime reports. This schema allows us to reflect upon the economics of publishing and cultural practices as well as locate Jack in the appropriate discourses of his time. Jack and his extraordinary longevity as a cultural phenomenon allow us to reflect upon memory, practice, and consumption in a narrative age that often dines out on crime. The irrelevant quirky criminology will be revisited every time the crimes are brought into narratives and analysis. There, I spiral and volute as a worm-eaten-upright-walking-cadaver, snickering, festering, bristling with irony; in that slippage of 'criminology' for 'truism', time's index finger stockades me, the dead, the events, and my prose together as 'crime report'... lose the Lodz for a jiffy and the exclusive history and diegesis of criminology's primary trans-generational genre – please! – let me spin! The section devoted to the crimes of Fallada, the warden's wife Emily, and the cadelskeschern is part polemic, part manifesto.

One of the principal difficulties with researching the crimes of 1888 is that debate focuses upon interpretation of, and access to, archival sources. At the time, police reportage "presented a distorted and partial view of events; they were concerned with the retrieval of offenders and property". Advances in technology now enable increased access to this material, yet the most accurate information about the victims, the murder scenes, and the crimes themselves is the most difficult to obtain. To this end, there are specific divisions regarding interpretation of the Ripper case. The status of the women killed by Jack is a key issue in the debates, as is interpretation of the terms 'prostitution', 'brothels', and 'vice' throughout the East End of London at the time of the murders. Albeit not peripheral to this study, the debate over the identity and motives of Jack the Ripper is beyond the scope of the current study.

CHAPTER 10

Conclusion

Following the surprising revelation that Oscar Wilde was Britain's most famous murderer, Jack the Ripper, this study explored the significance of this confession against some of the more traditional solutions to this enduring enigma. The confession entitled "The Real Cabman: The Real Jack the Ripper" was written by 31-year-old journalist Charles Johnston and published in the Nottinghamshire Guardian in July 1895. Wilde's authorship of "The Real Cabman" was exposed shortly afterwards and the confession was widely reported across the United Kingdom. Indeed, the degree of controversy ensures it an important place within the case's very vast document history.

Having reviewed a selection of these documents, we have become convinced that Wilde's confession both reshapes and transforms our current knowledge of Jack the Ripper. Indeed, we are more than confident that in the figure of Britain's greatest murderer, we have finally discovered the one person solely responsible for this series of brutal atrocities. That Jack the Ripper was in fact the Irish-born, London-based journalist who at the time of the crimes was aged 24 and answering to his Sunday name of William. Furthermore, that he wrote a heart-rending letter reporting these slayings to The Times. The veracity of which was strikingly vouchsafed, however inadvertently, by his wife in her ill-fated Libel trial of 1913. We also remain equally convinced that Wilde's punishment for these foul abominations is the sole mystery of his biography still obstinately to resist our earnest intellectual goodwill.

Final Thoughts and Reflections

Over the past 130 years or so, the world has been gripped by the Whitechapel murders, and the prospect of identifying, without a shadow of a doubt, the world's most notorious and enigmatic villain is one of the most exciting prospects conceivable. To be able to finally confirm without doubt his identity separates the fantasy from reality. It gives the Ripper a three-dimensionality that we have never really been able to assign to him across the centuries. These secrets and revelations are of monumental consequence to criminologists and individuals who are fascinated with the case and all its minute details. They confirm with absolute certainty what for years we could only speculate. They ground the Ripper in history to the precise date of 2:35 p.m. on December 13th, 2018, at which point his true identity was unveiled to the world. Has that ever been done in the case before?

For me, the Penn ending represents a poetic, fitting conclusion to this essay on the Ripper and his world. Having presented all my primary sources and the evidence against them, having walked the reader through it so that they can see it for themselves, I wanted to finally spell out to them in black and white where I stand. I happen to believe that Jack the Ripper was Herman Webster Mudgett, more famously known as Dr. Henry Howard Holmes, or H. H. Holmes. If I'm wrong, hey, I'm wrong, but I am convinced to the very bottom of my soul that the world's most notorious sadist and psychopath, the first of the modern serial killers, was none other than this New England murderer and grifter extraordinaire of the mid-19th century. And what this essay demonstrates especially is how I came to those conclusions.